'Incredible, informative, very powerful... I felt so
touched by it and changed by it... I can't recommend
it highly enough... A beautiful piece of work'
Jonathan Ross, BBC Radio 2

'A book for our times'
Mark Lawson, *Guardian*, Books of the Year

'Defiant and powerful... Leiris shows us,
poignantly and movingly, how the absence of
Hélène opens up for him and his son'
The Times

'One of the most enduring and memorable
messages after the deadly attack on Paris's Bataclan
theatre was written by journalist Antoine Leiris.
This bracing, courageous, and utterly beautiful
book shows us that he had much more to say'
Elle

'The man whose words have inspired millions'
BBC News

'This is a soliloquy not only on grief but on love,
a raw but controlled cry of fury and defiance
against a senseless killing, and a touching addition
to the rich tradition of writing about loss'
Times Literary Supplement

'It is simple and immediate, and is all about love and loss... An astonishing feat'
Sunday Times

'Poignant'
Grazia

'A beautifully written memoir... It's the hardest book you can pick up this year, but also the most affecting'
GQ

'Very intimate and full of love'
Belfast Telegraph

'Tissues at the ready, because though this book be little, it is FIERCE... No fluff. No forgiveness. No forgetting. I read it in one brief sitting, lying in the bath, tears dripping into the water'
The Pool

'This book is a love song to Hélène, a promise to Melvil and a resolution not to be defeated by chaos and barbarity. It is a stunning mission statement'
Irish Times

'An extraordinarily moving book'
Mirror

ANTOINE LEIRIS

A former cultural commentator for France Info and France Bleu, Antoine Leiris is a journalist in Paris. *You Will Not Have My Hate* is his first book.

ANTOINE LEIRIS

You Will Not
Have My Hate

TRANSLATED FROM THE FRENCH BY
Sam Taylor

VINTAGE

1 3 5 7 9 10 8 6 4 2

Vintage
20 Vauxhall Bridge Road,
London SW1V 2SA

Vintage is part of the Penguin Random House group of companies
whose addresses can be found at global.penguinrandomhouse.com.

Penguin
Random House
UK

Copyright © Antoine Leiris 2016

English translation copyright © Sam Taylor 2016

Antoine Leiris has asserted his right to be identified as the
author of this Work in accordance with the Copyright,
Designs and Patents Act 1988

First published in Vintage in 2017
First published in hardback by Harvill Secker in 2016

First published with the title *Vous n'aurez pas ma haine* in
France by Librairie Arthème Fayard in 2016

penguin.co.uk/vintage

A CIP catalogue record for this book is available from
the British Library

ISBN 9781784705282

Printed and bound by Clays Ltd, St Ives plc

Penguin Random House is committed to a sustainable future
for our business, our readers and our planet. This book is made
from Forest Stewardship Council® certified paper.

MIX
Paper from
responsible sources
FSC
www.fsc.org   FSC® C018179

'I've looked everywhere for her.'

'. . .'

'Is there anyone left in there?'

'Monsieur, you should prepare yourself
for the worst.'

YOU WILL NOT HAVE MY HATE

ONE NIGHT
IN HELL

Melvil fell asleep without a murmur, as he usually does when his mama isn't there. He knows that with Papa, the lullabies are not as soft and the hugs not as warm, so he doesn't expect too much.

To keep myself awake until she gets home, I read. The story of a novelist-turned-detective who discovers that a novelist-turned-murderer did not actually write the novel that made him want to become a novelist. After twist upon twist, I find out that the novelist-turned-murderer did not actually murder anyone. Much ado about nothing. My phone, lying on my bedside table, buzzes. I read the text:

'HEY, EVERYTHING OK? ARE YOU AT HOME?'

I don't want to be disturbed. I hate those text messages that don't really say anything. I don't reply.

'EVERYTHING OK?'

'. . .'

'ARE YOU SAFE?'

What's that supposed to mean, 'safe'? I put the book down and rush to the living room on tiptoes. *Do not wake the baby.* I grab the remote. The box of horrors takes for ever to come on. Live: Terrorist attack at the Stade de France. The images tell me nothing. I think about Hélène. I should call her, tell her it would be a good idea to take a taxi home. But there is something else. In the corridors of the stadium, some people stand frozen in front of a screen.

I do not see the images on that screen, only the expressions on the people's faces. They look appalled. They are watching something that I can't see. Not yet. Then, at the bottom of my screen, the news on the ticker that slides past too fast suddenly stops. The end of innocence.

'Terrorist attack at the Bataclan.'

The sound cuts out. All I can hear is the noise of my heart trying to burst out of my chest. Those five words seem to echo endlessly in my head. One second lasts a year. A year of silence, sitting there, on my couch. It must be a mistake. I check that that is where she went. Maybe I got it mixed up, or forgot. But the concert really is at the Bataclan. Hélène is at the Bataclan.

The picture cuts out. I can't see anything now, but I feel an electric shock go through my body. I want to run outside, to steal a car, to go out and look for her. The only thing in my head now is this burning sense of urgency. Only movement can put out those flames. But I am paralysed because Melvil is with me. I am trapped here. Condemned to watch as the fire spreads. I want to scream, but it's impossible. *Do not wake the baby.*

I grab my phone. I have to call her, talk to her, hear her voice. Contacts. 'Hélène', just Hélène. I never changed her name in my contacts list, never added 'my love' or a photo of the two of us. Neither did she. The call she never received that night was from 'Antoine L.' It rings out. Goes to voicemail. I hang up, I call again. Once, twice, a hundred times. However many it takes.

I feel suffocated by this couch that seems to be swallowing me up. The whole flat is collapsing in on me. At each unanswered call, I sink a little deeper into the ruins. Everything looks unfamiliar. The world around me fades. There is nothing left but her and me. A phone call from my brother brings me back to reality.

'Hélène is there.'

In the moment when I pronounce these words, I realise there is no way out. My brother and sister come to our flat. No one knows what to say.

There is nothing to say. There is no name for this. In the living room, the TV is on. We wait, eyes riveted to the twenty-four-hour news channels, which have already begun competing to come up with the most lurid, grotesque headline, the one that will keep us watching, spectators to a world that is falling apart. 'Massacre', 'carnage', 'bloodbath'. I turn off the TV before the word 'slaughter' can be uttered. The window on the world is closed. Reality returns.

N.'s wife calls me. He was at the Bataclan with Hélène. He's safe. I call him, he doesn't answer. Once. Twice. Three times. Finally, he picks up. He says he doesn't know where she is. Hélène's mother joins us.

I have to act, do something. I need to go outside, quickly, so I can find her, so I can escape the army of unspoken words that have invaded my living room. My brother clears the way for me. Without a word, he picks up his car keys. We confer in whispers. Close the door quietly behind us. *Do not wake the baby.*

The ghost hunt can begin.

———

There's silence in the car. In the city around us, too. From time to time, the painful screams of a siren disturb the hush that has descended on Paris. The party is over. The fanfare has ended. We go to all the major hospitals, anywhere that might be taking in the wounded. Bichat, Saint-Louis, Salpêtrière, Georges-Pompidou . . . That night, death has spread to all four corners of France's capital. One of its ticket-sellers awaits me at each stop. 'I'm looking for my wife. She was at the Bataclan.' Her name is not on any of the lists. But each time, they give me what I'm looking for: a new reason to keep going. 'Not all the wounded have been identified yet.' 'They're taking survivors at Bichat too.' 'Some of them have even been taken to hospitals in the suburbs.' I leave my mobile number, knowing that they will not call me back. Run to the car. I miss the silence of the road.

The streetlights speed past by the side of the ring road. The night deepens. Each light brings me one step closer to hypnosis. My body is no longer mine.

My mind is on the road. If I keep going around and around this too-tight belt that suffocates the city in its grip, something will eventually happen.

———

Even when there was nothing left to look for, we kept going. I needed to escape. To get away as far as possible, not to turn back. To keep going to the end of the road . . . to see if there is an end to it, an end to all of this.

I saw it, the end of the road.

It shone from the screen of my mobile phone when my alarm went off. Seven o'clock in the morning.

———

In half an hour, Melvil will drink from his bottle. He must still be sleeping. A baby's sleep, uncluttered by the horrors of the world.

Time to go home.

'Take the Porte de Sèvres exit . . .'

WAITING

Melvil waits. He waits to be big enough to reach the light switch in the living room. He waits to be well behaved enough to go out without a buggy. He waits for me to make his dinner before I read him a story. He waits for bath time, for lunchtime, for snack time. And tonight, he waits for his mother to come home before he goes to bed. Waiting is a feeling without a name. As I read him one last story, it brings all of them at the same time. It is distress, hope, sadness, relief, surprise, dread.

I wait too. To be sentenced. A few angry men have delivered their verdict with automatic gunfire. For us, it will be a life sentence. But I still don't know that. We sing a song before bedtime. I tell myself she will come through the bedroom door and join us for the last couplet. I tell myself she will finally call. I tell myself we are going to wake up soon.

Melvil has fallen asleep. The telephone rings. It's Hélène's sister.

'Antoine, I'm so sorry . . .'

THE LADYBIRD

15 November
5 p.m.

After the walk, it's time for Melvil to settle down.
Later will come bath time, dinner time, and then,
finally, bedtime. Today, I can tell he is annoyed. His
pain, still speechless, shows through in every little
worry of his infant life. The biscuit is too soft; he
doesn't want to eat it. The ball has rolled too far;
he doesn't want to play any more. The straps on his
buggy are too tight; he doesn't want to stay in there.
He struggles with everything jostling inside him,
everything that he doesn't understand. An unspeak-
able turmoil that robs him of the innocent curiosity
of a little boy. What is this feeling that makes him

want to cry when he's not hungry, not in pain, not afraid? He misses his mother. She hasn't come home for two days now. She'd never been away for more than a single evening before.

To soothe him, I send him to find a book from his bedroom. His bookshelf is low enough for him to reach the books himself, populated with characters named after the feelings they embody: Mr Happy, Mr Silly, Mr Grumpy . . . There is also an elephant who really wants to grow up. A little cloth mouse into which I fit my finger, and who, page after page, tries to escape the cat chasing it. Finally, the mouse hides in a flowerpot and asks for a goodnight kiss, which Melvil never refuses it.

Today, smiling his six-tooth smile, he returns from his mission with a book that he likes to read with his mother. It is the story of a pretty little ladybird in an enchanted garden. All the insects who gather nectar there admire the ladybird because she is so good-hearted. She is the prettiest and kindest of all the insects. Her mama is so proud of her. But, one day, the little ladybird lands by chance on the hooked nose of an evil witch.

Melvil has never known that the witch turns this sweet ladybird into a nasty ladybird. Concerned that he might be scared by them, Hélène always skipped those pages where the flying red-and-black beetle – with a spider and a toad for accomplices – terrorised the usually tranquil garden. The ladybird that Melvil heard about every night never landed on that witch's nose.

Snug in his bed, he only saw the good fairy who, with a wave of her magic wand, made the little insect beautiful and kind again. Today, I skip those pages too. But when I see the fairy appear, in her dream-blue, star-covered dress, smiling the serene smile of one who already knows how the story ends, I suddenly stop.

Melvil will not be able to skip these pages of his life the way he skipped the pages of the story. I have no magic wand. Our little ladybird landed on the witch's nose. The witch had a Kalashnikov and death at its fingertip.

I have to tell him, now. But how?

Mama, papa, milk. Melvil can only say three words, but he understands everything. Yet if I sit down with him and say, 'Mama's had a serious accident. She won't ever be able to come home,' that would be using adult words to tell him a grown-up story. He wouldn't be able to grasp what it means to him beyond those words. It would be like killing her a second time. Words are not enough.

He gets annoyed, stamps his feet, throws his books on the floor. He's about to have a meltdown. I pick up my phone to play the songs that he listens to with her, with his thumb in his mouth, wrapping himself around her like an affectionate little boa constrictor.

I hold him against my body, trap him between my legs, so he can feel me, understand me. He spent nine months inside his mother, listening to her live: her heartbeat was the rhythm of his days, her movements were his journey, her words the music of his nascent life. I want him to hear, his ear to my chest, my voice telling him my sorrow. I want him to feel my muscles tensed by the gravity of this moment.

I want the beating of my heart to reassure him: life will go on.

On the phone, I find the playlist that his mother put together for him, and hit play.

She hand-picked every single song, as if each one were a sort of musical bridge between his baby's ears and the harmonies of the grown-up world. Henri Salvador and his 'Chanson Douce' rub shoulders with Françoise Hardy's 'Temps de l'Amour'. An ode to the moon lights up 'Berceuse à Frédéric' by Bourvil. As the first notes of this song play, I open the Photos folder. Her face appears, blurred, badly framed, but that is all it takes to jolt Melvil from the fragile calm produced by the opening words of the song. 'It's time to sleep now . . . my little Frédéric . . . I found this music . . . that I give you like a present . . . at the bottom of your cradle.'

Immediately he points an anxious finger towards her, and then turns to me, his smile turned upside down and warm tears welling in his eyes. I break down, and I explain to him as best I can that his mama will not be able to come home, that she had a serious accident, that it's not her fault, she would have loved to be with him, but she can't any more. He cries like I've never seen him cry before. He's shed a few tears before, of course, out of pain, fear, disappointment, tantrums.

But this, this is something else altogether. This is his first real sorrow. The first time he has ever felt true sadness.

The photographs flash up one by one, and the music starts to sting. We are like two children, leaning over a music box that plays the tune of our life, crying our little hearts out. It's normal that you feel sad; you're allowed to be sad, Papa is sad too. Whenever you feel like this, come to see me and we'll look at the photos. The song ends. 'Don't forget this music . . . that I gave you one day . . . with all my love . . .' The memories slowly take away some of the hurt. The parade of photographs becomes a game. That's Melvil, that's Mama. It doesn't matter. We'll have to talk about it again soon anyway.

The tale of the little ladybird ends when, having once again become the prettiest ladybird in the garden, she finds her mama, who cries with joy at seeing her little girl again.

Telling him is only the first step on the long path that awaits us. The witch has gone, but now I must explain to him, every time he needs to hear it, why his mama will not be waiting for him at the end of his story.

I tear the page out of the book and pin it to the wall of his bedroom, next to a photograph of her. Melvil is holding on to her shoulders while he lies on her back. Her smile is like a flash of spring sunshine. A lock of hair falls over her eyes.

She is looking at me, no pose, no lens. Her eyes speak directly to me. They tell me about the simple joys of those seventeen months we spent together, the three of us.

IT COULD HAVE
BEEN . . .

16 November
9.30 a.m.

Melvil is at nursery. It's Monday morning, at a bar in the fifteenth arrondissement. People have grey faces and broken dreams. The television is tuned to BFM, and all available eyes are glued to the screen, looking for something to talk about, now that the usual conversational topics – rising taxes, the flu – are worn out. It's Monday, but no one can talk about anything but last Friday.

'A double espresso!'

I have to go to see Hélène this morning at the police mortuary. Next to me, two men, aged between forty-five and fifty, with the weary eyes of those who've seen too much, are discussing what I don't want to hear. There is no way to avoid a conversation when you sit at the bar, it just happens to you. This would normally be a pleasure, to sit alone and, for the time it takes to drink a coffee, to overhear these bits and pieces of other people's lives. But today, it is my life that is in bits and pieces.

Even though I turn away, trying not to hear, a few words reach me through the hissing steam of the espresso machine.

'. . . can't let all those people die for nothing . . .'

Does anyone ever really die for anything?

It could have been a reckless driver who forgot to brake, a tumour that was slightly more malignant than the others, or a nuclear bomb. The only thing that matters is that she's no longer here. Guns, bullets, violence – all of this is just background noise to the real tragedy now taking place: absence.

Not many people understand how I can so quickly get over the circumstances in which Hélène was killed. People ask me if I've forgotten or forgiven. I forgive nothing, I forget nothing. I am not getting over anything, and certainly not so quickly. When everyone else has gone back to his or her life, we will still be living with this. This story is our story. To refuse it would be to betray it. Even if her disfigured body is corpse-cold, even if her kiss tastes like still-warm blood, and even if what she whispers into my ear has the chilling beauty of a funeral requiem, I have to hold her to me. I have to be a part of this story.

Of course, having a culprit, someone to take the brunt of your anger, is an open door, a chance to temporarily escape your suffering. And the more odious the crime, the more ideal the culprit, the more legitimate your hatred. You think about him in order not to think about yourself. You hate him in order not to hate what's left of your life. You rejoice at his death in order not to have to smile at those who remain.

Perhaps these are aggravating circumstances – to say the least. But aggravating circumstances are for trials, as a way of quantifying loss. But people do not count their tears, and they certainly don't dry them on the sleeves of their anger. Those with no one to blame are alone with their grief. I am one of them. Alone with my son, who will soon ask me what happened that night. What would I be telling him if I placed the responsibility for the circumstances of our life at someone else's feet? If it was to those men that he had to turn in order to make sense of things? Death awaited his mother that night; they were merely ambassadors.

With a burst of machine gun fire, they shattered our puzzle. And after we have put it back together, piece by piece, it will no longer be the same. There will be someone missing in the picture, there will be only the two of us, but we will take up the whole picture. She will be with us, invisible, but there. It is in our eyes that you will read her presence, in our joy that her flame will burn, in our veins that her tears will flow.

We will never return to our life of before. But we will not build a life against them. We will move forward in our own life.

'Another double espresso, please, and the bill!'

'Crazy, what happened, isn't it?' one of the men says to me.

'I haven't had time to think about it, really. My wife wasn't around this weekend, and I had my baby with me. But I'm going to see her now.'

SEEING HER AGAIN

16 November
10 a.m.

They should hand out fluorescent vests to everyone I want to avoid. The psychological support staff are wearing them this morning, which makes my task easier. I don't want to talk to them. I have the impression they want to steal from me. To take my misery and apply a balm of formulaic phrases that will leave me insipid, watered down, without poetry, without beauty.

So I map out the premises. Colour-coded. Blue, police, so I can get through. Fluorescent yellow, psychological support staff, to avoid. Black, mortuary staff, so I can see her again. I head towards someone in blue, who leads me to someone in black, who suggests I go to see someone in fluorescent yellow. I pretend not to hear what he says. I am accompanied by Hélène's mother and sister. It takes for ever to get there. A few metres are like an eternity.

Long needles of icy rain streak our faces. Every person I see follows the script to the letter. An actor in a play repeated over and over again, a mournful vaudeville, a worn-out comedy.

Death is on the playbill today, and yet this walk is not a funeral procession. It isn't time for that. This is a happy day, the return of a loved one.

Inside the building, the tiles look old and shabby. So do the employees' faces. It's cold. Since arriving, I have been asked a dozen times if I would like to sit down; each time, I refuse, out of fear that I won't be able to get up again. I wait, standing up.

Protocols. Paperwork. Families come and go. About fifteen enter before us. All re-emerge in pieces.

'You've come to see Luna-Hélène Muyal?'

It's our turn.

The room where we are led is more warmly decorated. Death's waiting room is not as I imagined it. And yet, behind the polished boards that cover the room's walls from floor to ceiling, I hear the blood of the dead flowing. From one moment to the next, I imagine it seeping through the wood panelling and slowly flooding the room. Climbing from our feet to our heads. Drowning us in a bloodbath. In truth, we are drowning already.

A young woman speaks to us. She has done this a thousand times before, I can hear it in her voice. 'Difficult moments . . . terrible circumstances . . . police work . . .' All these words sound worn out, a second-hand compassion. Her silences are calculated, her gestures prepared, her smile looks like it's straight from the *Illustrated Undertaker's Handbook*. 'Chapter Five: Talking to the Family.'

I am just one among so many others.

I only half listen to her. Hélène is there, just next door. I can sense her. I would like to see her, alone.

Hélène's mother and sister understand. They know that, even here, it is the two of us, first of all. Together for this final moment, just her and me. Not someone's daughter, or sister, or best friend, not the woman who was killed at the Bataclan. I want her to be mine, and mine alone. As she was before.

We were like two little Lego bricks that fitted together perfectly. Made for each other. Our 'once upon a time' began one 21 June, with music, at a concert. As always happens at the start of the great stories, I thought she wouldn't want someone like me. I thought she was too beautiful, too Parisian, too sophisticated, too everything, for a nobody like me. I took her hand. We were swallowed up by the crowd and the noise. Until the last moment, I thought she would escape me. Then we kissed.

Afterwards, it all happened very fast. I told her we would go to New York, that the time belonged to us, that my lucky star would guide us. She told me she loved me.

A love story like any other. We were just sane enough to realise how lucky we were, and crazy enough to gamble everything on it. That love was our treasure.

The door opens.

'Let me know when you're ready.'

She is there. I move towards her, turn around, check that we are alone. This moment is ours. A pane of Perspex separates us. I press on it with all my weight. Our life together flashes before my eyes. I feel as though I never had another life. Hélène was the moon. A brunette with milk-white skin, eyes that made her look like a frightened owl, a smile you could fit the whole world inside. I remember her smile on our wedding day.

But the most beautiful moments of our lives are not those we stick in photograph albums. I remember all those moments when we just took the time to love each other. Seeing an old couple and wanting to be like them. A burst of laughter. An empty morning, lounging in the comfort of our sheets.

It is the most insignificant moments, where there is nothing to show, nothing to tell, that are the most beautiful. Those are the ones that fill my memory.

She is just as beautiful as she always was.

When you close a dead person's eyes, you give them back a little bit of life. She looks like the woman I watched wake up each morning. I want to lie next to her languorous body, warm her up, tell her she is the most beautiful woman I ever met. I want to close my eyes too and wait for Melvil to call out to us, wait for him to start tangling himself up in our crumpled sheets.

Hélène often asked me if love could be shared. If, after the arrival of our child, I would still love her as much. After his birth, she never asked that question again.

I cry, I talk to her. I would like to stay another hour, at least a day, perhaps a lifetime. But I must leave her. The moon must set. Today, 16 November, the sun rises on our new 'once upon a time'. The story of a father and a son who go on living alone, without the aid of the star to whom they swore allegiance.

'Monsieur, it is time to leave her . . .'

THE MUSIC
CAN BEGIN

16 November
11 a.m.

I have just come out of the mortuary. It did me good
to see her. For two days, she was alone in the deep
night that the terrorists had brought down on Paris.
The City of Light was extinguished at the same
moment that her eyes were closed. Such big eyes that
saw the world in its entirety. Such big eyes that will
never see her son get up again.

Since coming out of the mortuary, I have only
one thought in my head: going to see Melvil at the
nursery. Finding him and telling him that I saw his
mother and I brought her with me. I brought

him back his mama, she's not lost any more, she is in the palm of my hand and she will come home with us.

But I must have a coffee with Hélène's family to talk about what happens next: the funeral, the police, the psychological support . . . All those bureaucratic irritations that pollute grief. You imagine your grief as something pure, free of all material contingencies, but the reality of a burial quickly takes over. You don't even have time to take stock of what has happened to you before the parade of *sorry*s in black suits has already begun.

'You have to go to the funeral home. If you want, I can help you.'

Silence.

Since Friday evening, I had practically lost the ability to speak. Sentences of more than three words tired me out. I was exhausted by the idea of putting words together, of putting thoughts into words. In any case, I was incapable of thinking.

In my head, there was her, whom I hadn't seen again, and him, whom I had to look after, and that buzzing noise that scrambled all the rest. I responded with silence, even to simple questions. At best, some people were answered with grunts of varying lengths and tones, sounds that they had to decipher to understand if I was hungry, if I wanted them to stay with me tonight, if I wanted a light for my cigarette. Since seeing her today, the buzzing has started to fade and my tongue to loosen.

'You'll have to be careful not to get ripped off, compare prices. We can come with you if you want!'

'I'll take care of it on my own.'

'Some people take advantage of others dying to try to scam their relatives!'

Time to go. I have to pick up the baby.

———

We are in the car, on the way back, when it begins. My brother-in-law, who is driving us, sees my foot frenetically tapping the floor of the car, and says re-assuringly: 'You'll get to the nursery on time, don't worry.'

It is not the stress of being late that dictates these movements, it is the words imposing their rhythm. One after another or all at the same time. They go in, some come out, some clash, those that remain call to others, and each one begins to play a few notes. Like the moments before an orchestra starts to play. You hear scattered sounds, dissonant, ran-dom, and then suddenly the notes blend together and climb up your spine, louder and louder until ab-solute silence. The music can begin.

I am happy to see him again. My smile as I open the door of the nursery collides with an army of em-barrassed faces and dangling arms. He stands there, in the middle of what looks like a Napoleonic legion during a retreat from Russia.

Melvil was the only one, that day, who could re-spond to my smile with a smile. The only one, that day, who saw that I had his mama with me. We go home on the path that he adores, the one where we see the most road signs – which are one of the things he's passionate about, along with books, music and the obsessive closing of doors. He lifts up his arms: 'No parking!' He lifts them again less than fifteen metres later . . . another 'No parking!' And so on . . .

House, lunch, nappy, pyjamas, nap, computer. The words continue to arrive. They come on their own, considered, weighed, but without me having to summon them. They come to me. All I have to do is pluck them from the air.

I chose each one, brought them together, separated them sometimes, and – after a few minutes as an intermediary – the letter is there: 'You will not have my hate.'

I hesitate for a while before posting it, then my brother forces me to do what I have not done for two days.

'Lunch is ready. Come and eat!'

No time to think about it. No desire to come back to it. Facebook, through which I'm communicating with some of Hélène's friends whose phone numbers I don't have, is open in the next tab. 'What's on your mind?' it asks. Copy, paste, post. My words no longer belong to me.

'YOU WILL NOT HAVE MY HATE'

*On Friday night, you stole the life of an
exceptional being, the love of my life, the mother
of my son, but you will not have my hate. I don't
know who you are and I don't want to know. You
are dead souls. If that God for whom you blindly
kill made us in his image, each bullet in my
wife's body will have been a wound in his heart.*

*So, no, I will not give you the satisfaction of
hating you. That is what you want, but to
respond to your hate with anger would be to yield
to the same ignorance that made you what you
are. You want me to be scared, to see my fellow
citizens through suspicious eyes, to sacrifice my
freedom for security. You have failed. I will not
change.*

I saw her this morning. At last, after days and nights of waiting. She was as beautiful as she was when she went out on Friday evening, as beautiful as when I fell madly in love with her more than twelve years ago. Of course I am devastated by grief, I grant you that small victory, but it will be short-lived. I know she will be with us every day and that we will see each other in the paradise of free souls to which you will never have access.

There are only two of us — my son and myself — but we are stronger than all the armies of the world. Anyway, I don't have any more time to waste on you, as I must go to see Melvil, who is just waking up from his nap. He is only seventeen months old. He will eat his snack as he does every day, then we will play as we do every day, and all his life this little boy will defy you by being happy and free. Because you will not have his hate either.

THE MASTER
OF TIME

17 November
10.45 a.m.

The doorbell rings.

I am not expecting anyone. I look through the peephole. There's a man at the door. His ears stick out. That is the only distinguishing feature of his face. His eyes, his mouth, his nose, all the rest, seem to have been deliberately designed to allow him to go about unnoticed. He is somehow everyone and no one at the same time. I open the door.

'Hello, monsieur . . .'

He is dressed in a worn grey uniform. A clip-board in his right hand, with a sheet of paper clipped to it. I look him up and down, indifferent. He stares at me, slightly embarrassed. Then finally he says:

'I've come to read the electric meter.'

I should have remembered the letter warning me of this visit. Hélène stuck it to our fridge, and I walk past the fridge several times a day. But recently I have been blind to the world.

'Can I come in?'

I thought that if the moon ever disappeared, the sea would retreat so no one would see it crying. I thought the winds would stop dancing. That the sun would not want to rise again.

Nothing of the kind. The world continues to turn, and meters must be read.

Silently, I move out of the way. Watch him walk ahead of me. He enters our flat with his big, clumpy boots, his stride of the living. I do not tell him where the meter is. He knows what to do. He has already done it ten times today, maybe a thousand times this week. It's all he has done his whole life. I watch him work, from a distance. I want to tell him that this is not a good time. He's not welcome here. He has just screamed into my ears that, in the world outside, life goes on. And I don't want to hear that.

Since Friday, the only master of time has been Melvil. He is the conductor of the symphony of our days. Waking, eating, napping, snacking. No matter what time it is, he decides when the universe must rise, and I adapt in order to keep his world intact. Every day I play the same melody, keeping time with his metronome, taking care not to miss a single note. Get up. Hug. Breakfast. Play. Go for a walk. Music. Lunch. Stories. Hug. Nap. Get up again. Snack. Go for another walk. Shopping. Music. Bath. Dinner. Stories. Hug. Sleep.

It is the only way I have found to tell him that life continues, regardless. Clinging to our habits is a way of shutting out the terrible and the wonderful. The horror of that night, and the compassion that followed at its heels. The wound, and the bandages that people wanted to heal it with. Neither has any place in our already full little life.

Sometimes the barriers fall. Quietly. Behind 'Come on, it's time for your snack', Melvil detects the hint of a repressed sob. My heart is beating too fast. He knows that Papa is sad. He sees the gaping hole appear in our life. An invisible monster comes out to drag us down there. We cry. Slowly, the hole closes up. We are still here. The orchestra conductor and his soloist. Our little carousel goes around and around every day, endlessly.

That man checking the meter in the kitchen is a false note. I watch him, waiting for the moment when he will realise he is out of tune. He just carefully notes down the numbers on his sheet of paper. I want to throw him out. But I don't do anything of the kind. I stay in the doorway and bow down before the world as it continues to turn. Before life, which enters our flat in spite of my wishes.

Before those strangers, who remind me that I have no choice, that I am still alive.

'That's it, monsieur, all done.'

The door closes behind him. The music is in tune once again. Time to pick up Melvil from nursery.

HOME-MADE MEALS

18 November
11.30 a.m.

The nursery manager pulls me aside before Melvil and I can escape, dummy in his mouth, cigarette in mine.

'Salomé's mama brought some home-made soup for you . . .'

Since Hélène died, strangers from all over the world have offered to look after my son, we've been invited to go on holidays in every continent on the planet, we've been sent socks, a hat, gifts, and cheques that I have never deposited.

The other nursery mothers moved into action on Tuesday morning. Still whole in their maternity, they cannot bear to imagine us, two poor young guys alone in a big house without Mama. They have found a way to help us without Melvil or I having anything to say about it.

Every day, when I open the door of the nursery, I hear: 'Whose mama?' I'm Melvil's papa. And because our children are the same age, because they know how hard it is to raise a baby, because they know the ties that bind a mother to her children, what they see in me is the man, the papa who will never be a mama. The man who will never manage, alone, with a baby. I see concern in their eyes. Where everyone else imagines me as a super-papa, they know that I am a simple papa.

'Shall I put it in a bag?'

I expect to see a little glass jar. Instead she takes a gigantic Tupperware box from the fridge, filled to the brim with a carrot–potato–squash soup blended with care.

'Tomorrow, Yana's mama will bring you something.'

That was how it began.

We went home, the two of us, with our gigantic box of soup. The next day, when I picked up Melvil, I was handed another Tupperware, this time filled with carrot–pumpkin–spinach soup.

Then the brigade of mothers mobilised. Too many offers for the little belly of a seventeen-month-old boy. They had to get organised. Each one taking her turn.

On Thursday, coming out of the nursery, I had not one but two little glass pots in my bag. Manon's mama had meticulously covered the first with a little square of cloth on which she had written the soup's ingredients. Carrot–pumpkin–green beans. Around the second, she had noted on a sheet of paper: 'Puree of broccoli, potatoes, corn, garlic, and minced lamb.' She must have started over several times, carefully choosing the colour of the lids and the little elastic bands that hold the menus in place. As if everything she wanted to give us, give me, overflowed from this too-small pot and ended up in this origami bird that she left inside the bag. As if she had wanted to be there at the moment when I opened it. As if she had wanted to make sure that – even after that, even after that – my insides were looked after. 'Bon appétit, Melvil – from Manon and her mama.'

Friday's pot is from Victor's mama. Her speciality is the lightly caramelised apple–pear compote. Inside the bag, next to this meal, is a note bearing words of comfort: 'Dear Antoine and Melvil, you can count on me.'

Friday is also the day when I am supposed to return the containers. The nursery manager, who is in charge of planning the meal schedule, explains how things work to me. Everything must be washed, dried and put in the little bag, which I will pick up again on Monday, when I leave the nursery with Melvil.

So things were organised like that. Without a word from me, the nursery mothers got together to ensure that, every day, Melvil ate meals made with a mama's love.

When Hélène was pregnant, we swore we would be the best parents in the world. We settled for being good parents, in particular abandoning our culinary ambitions. Melvil got used to supermarket meals. The first spoonful of soup made by 'Salomé's mama' ended up on the floor. Second spoon, pyjamas. Third spoon, wall. That will be the last.

Melvil never ate a single one of those home-made meals. I emptied the Tupperware boxes into the sink. After washing them, I took them back, and told them that Melvil had eaten it all.

'Did Melvil like his soup?' After a little nod of affirmation, slightly embarrassed by my white lie, I made sure to give a big smile of someone well fed, which pleased them. 'Yes, he ate every last mouthful.' And Melvil, at that moment, gave a little cry of disgust.

I let them keep this little game going as long as they needed to. They wanted to give a little of a mother's love to a child who was missing it so badly, and I took it. What did it matter if he actually ate the soup or not? I also understood that my son, although he would never have his own mother's love, would be given tenderness by all these others, in little pots full of puree.

I didn't have the courage to tell them that Melvil never tasted their home-made meals, and that the little pots could not stay in our house. Maybe this is because, even while still full, sitting on the dresser, those pots nourished our hearts with a sweet, maternal tenderness.

N.

19 November
9 p.m.

N. wrote to me tonight. We haven't talked since I told him about Hélène's death. He wants to see me. I wait for him at a table on a terrace. Around me, the usual hubbub of a Parisian café on a weeknight. As before. I spot his figure at the corner of the street. He is limping. He has a wound in his buttock, a souvenir of Friday's horror. I put on a suitable facial expression, then immediately change my mind. I don't want to play that game.

I take him in my arms. His is the biggest smile I have seen since Friday. A smile that cannot help but say, 'I'm alive.' Yes, he is alive. He sits down and, almost immediately, begins to tell me all about it. The start of the concert. The beer at the bar. The crowded mosh pit. And then the gunfire. The noises, the smells, the bodies. He doesn't spare me a single detail, he can't stop, he forces me to watch on fast forward the film that stole my life from me.

I called him that night, ten times, a hundred times, a thousand times. Probably while it was happening. Probably after. And when, at last, he picked up, I just wanted him to tell me that she was okay. That everything was okay. That she was with him. That maybe she was wounded, but she would survive. I wanted him to tell me that they'd been able to escape and run through the Parisian night. I imagined I could already hear the nervous laughter of two survivors. I waited for him to wake me from my nightmare.

'I can't tell you anything.'

A silence as heavy as the words he speaks to me now, at this café. And, with that silence, the horizon of doubt spread all over. The darkest despair and the craziest hope. Hélène, at once dead and alive.

Now I know. So, between two events in the story of which he is the hero, I realise why he didn't tell me that night that she had died, in his arms. I realise he is not yet the survivor I see. He is still there, trapped in that scene that is still being played. And when he apologises for not having been able to tell me, I don't blame him. In his film, the characters don't die. But this is not his film. That night, 13 November, is the story of the moon that will never rise again. He doesn't know it yet.

Minute after minute, I become the story he is telling. I note the setting. Commit it to memory. I know that Melvil will soon ask me how Mama died, I know he will want to know everything. So I stay calm. I listen quietly, a spectator to the tragedy of my life that has already begun, which did not wait for its narrator.

When he has finished, we talk about this and that, trying to pretend that everything has not collapsed. We talk about his wound, about Melvil's naps, about his shop, which he has reopened. Suddenly everything feels so normal, almost happy, and for a moment it is as if we are teenagers again.

The beer glasses are empty. We promise never to leave each other's lives.

STAY STRONG . . .

20 November
10.10 a.m.

Now, when people ask me 'How are you?' they
don't expect the usual formulaic response: 'Fine,
and you?' – the tacit authorisation to move on to
another subject of conversation because everything
is fine.

With me, everyone knows that everything is
not fine, that after I give my response we will not
move on to today's weather, last night's TV show
or the latest office gossip. Today, when I am asked,
'How are you . . .', the delivery is slower, the 'are'
elongated to draw out the question and delay a

potentially embarrassing silence. The person's head leans, generally to the right, one eyebrow is raised, generally the left, and the person's mouth is pursed as if to say: 'I'm ready to hear everything.' Then there is the look that attempts to dive inside me like a child's hand dives into a sweetie jar, hoping to grab, right at the bottom, his favourite pink one. For me, the pink sweet is my grief.

People want to meet me, talk to me, touch me. I am a totem. Assessed, measured, quantified, as if there were a Richter scale of sadness and they felt sure that, with me, they were facing the Big One. One of those massive earthquakes that happen only one to five times a century. Magnitude 9. Description: 'Devastating.' Effects: 'Mass destruction of areas over a radius of more than a thousand kilometres around the epicentre.'

So I tried to give a reply as conventional as 'Fine, and you?' A reply that has the double advantage of ending, before it has even begun, the diagnosis of my emotional state, and giving back the initiative in the conversation to the person who started it. I ended up with the default option of 'As well as can be expected', which allowed me to descend one step on the scale. Magnitude 8. Description: 'Major.' Effects: 'Considerable damage of all buildings, up to dozens of kilometres from the epicentre.' But that is not enough.

So I give a reassuring smile. The same for everyone. Lips closed, one corner of my mouth lifting only slightly, the other a little bit more, my eyes creased. The effect is immediate. Magnitude 7. Description: 'Very strong.' Effects: 'May cause severe damage over a vast area; near the epicentre, only adapted buildings will survive.'

My 'As well as can be expected' is one of those buildings. It is that little hut that is photographed after the catastrophe, the one that is left miraculously standing while everything around it is in ruins. It may not be much to look at, but it's still there.

I keep up appearances. I take the other person by the hand, and reassure him by showing this cardboard city that acts as the set for the film of my life that I let people see. The streets are clean, the inhabitants peaceful, life seems to go on as normally as possible. But the buildings are only facades, the inhabitants merely extras, and behind this apparent normality, there is nothing, nothing at all. Except, perhaps, this anxiety. What will happen when everyone has moved on to another film? Will I be alone here in my abandoned set?

'I'm truly sorry for everything that's happened. Stay strong . . .'

I don't have a ready-made response for that. 'See you soon' is a promise; 'Take care of yourself', an invitation. But 'Stay strong' is a life sentence. After trying to relieve me of the weight of this grief during the time it takes to have a conversation, the other person hands it back to me, intact. Two little words that reduce my Cinecittà to ashes. Most conversations end like that. The facades fall to the ground, the extras leave the set, and I am unmasked.

THE FINGERTIP

21 November
5.30 p.m.

Half past five in the afternoon is a wretched time of day. A stray, pointless hour. The one we would like to erase. The walk is over. Dinner is not yet ready. Melvil is too excited to play. I am too tired to be attentive. We are bored. We avoid each other, gauge each other's mood. Who will give in first? We wish that time would speed up.

Half past six, at last.

'Bath time!'

Our faces light up when I proudly announce this. Bath time is a moment we love to share. Melvil is a little fish in an aquarium. I am the boy who sticks his nose to the glass to watch him swimming. Sometimes I dip my fingers in the water to play. He comes to the surface to nibble them, and wriggles with pleasure. The day's worries sink quickly to the bottom of the bath, creating a silt of fears, tears and vexations that whirl down the drain with the bathwater.

Without her, it is not the same. This was a moment for the three of us. A ritual. I held Melvil tight, while Hélène washed him. Afterwards we played, sang, sloshed and splashed around, we laughed.

Today, we don't laugh so much. We act as if. As if all this still had some meaning without her. Sometimes, I even half expect her. Tell myself that she will open the bathroom door and join us. Start singing again.

'Time to come out!'

My little fish squirms in my arms. He is upset. She was the one who took care of him when he came out of the bath, in a delicately choreographed dance. Her hands slid over his shameless little body. He wriggled his toes with happiness at being cuddled like that. She put her nose on his navel, which had been their link. He laughed like he did when he was tickled. She brushed his hair like a little girl brushing her doll's hair. His chest swelled with pride at all this attention she lavished on him. At the end of this dance, the two partners left each other with a kiss.

Tonight, I learn a new step. I have to cut his fingernails. I have never done it before. And this time I cannot wait for Hélène to return. I sit him on my lap. He doesn't flinch. With his little hand in mine, I move the scissors closer, unsure which finger to start with. He fidgets impatiently. I cut the first nail.

A cry pierces the silence.

I look at him to reassure myself. He looks at me, surprised. I was the one who cried out. I have cut off the tip of his thumb. I shouldn't have started with the thumb. I felt something jamming the blades, but kept pressing. I examine his hand. In fact, it's a bit of skin that I cut off. His thumb, which I imagined amputated, is intact, but the tip is skinned, raw. It's not bleeding. I put his thumb in my mouth. I feel as if it's his heart beating between my lips. A little heart, doubly wounded.

What if he thought I wanted to hurt him? That I did it on purpose! What if he was afraid of me now? Instinctively, I turn around. Look for her. She is not there to reassure me. Not there to guide me. Not there to take over for me.

The vertigo of solitude. There is only me. And I still have nine nails to go. I feel ashamed. I feel so small. Like a child who wanted to play at being Papa but who didn't know the rules. But this is a grown-up's game, and I have lost. I cut his thumb. I want to give up, to climb under the bed and hide. I long for those arms in which I too could cry. For those arms that would do what I am still too small to do. I'm not up to this.

He is still looking at me, more and more surprised. He is not crying. He is not afraid. He is there.

I am there. We are a team. Two adventurers. He is waiting for me to finish so he can play.

I try again, and I have the impression that he is guiding me. Look, Papa, you do it like this. And we get there. The nail clippings fall one by one to the floor.

THE RIGHT TO DOZE

22 November
9 a.m.

I have just dropped Melvil at nursery. He didn't cry. I move slightly to the side so he won't see me watching him, behind one of those windowpanes in the nursery's glass facade. It is like a big bowl where we can see the fish swimming around. Sometimes we tap on the glass to get them to notice us. He is already playing with his musical book. It is a journey, in the space of a few pages, around the world of instruments. The bandoneon played by a llama, the balalaika by a bear. A fox in a Venetian gondola plays the mandolin.

At the nursery, everyone knows. When I arrive each morning, every person I see wears a mask. The carnival of the dead. Even if I tell them the fable of a man who will not lose control, I cannot persuade them to take off the masks. I know that, for them, I am no longer me: I am a ghost, the ghost of Hélène.

Melvil is alive. Almost as soon as he gets there, the masks come off. He enters on tiptoe, says good-bye to me, smiles, and one burst of laughter is all it takes for the funeral faces to fall to the bottom of the toy chest.

It is time for me to go home.

I pick up the post before walking upstairs. The postbox is barely even open before a flock of envelopes escapes from it, paper in different shapes and sizes scattering on the floor around me. There are thick envelopes, containing very long letters, a whole life shared with me. There are Manila envelopes, filled with children's drawings for Melvil. There are simple postcards. For a moment, at least, words have replaced the little box's usual stack of bills.

I open the first envelope. Read the postcard inside it as I climb the stairs. Kind words sent from the United States. At the door of the flat, I pick up a note left by a neighbour: 'If you need me to help with your son, don't hesitate to ask. Your neighbour across the hall.'

I put the letters on the living room table. The colour of one of the envelopes catches my eye. An old-fashioned off-white. A missive from another age. The paper has a letterhead. The man's name is Philippe. I imagine a grey-haired gentleman sitting at his writing desk. I slip inside his words. He is reacting to the message I posted on Facebook. His letter is beautiful. I feel snug, curled up in this envelope, where the sun shines. Then, at the bottom of the page, like a signature, these words: 'You are the one who was hurt, and yet it is you who gives us courage.'

Watching from a distance, you always have the impression that the person who survives a disaster is a hero. I know I am not. I was struck by the hand of fate, that's all. It did not ask me what I thought first. It didn't try to find out if I was ready. It came to take

Hélène, and it forced me to wake up without her. Since then, I have been lost: I don't know where I'm going, I don't know how to get there. You can't really count on me. I think about Philippe, the author of this letter. I think about all the others who have written to me. I want to tell them that I feel dwarfed by my own words. Even if I try to convince myself that they are mine, I don't know if I will live up to them. From one day to the next, I might drown.

And suddenly, I am afraid. Afraid that I won't be able to meet people's expectations. Will I no longer have the right to lack courage? The right to feel angry. The right to be overwhelmed. The right to be tired. The right to drink too much and start smoking again. The right to see another woman, or not to see other women. The right not to love again, ever. Not to rebuild my life and not to want a new life. The right not to feel like playing, going to the park, telling a story. The right to make mistakes. The right to make bad decisions. The right to not have time. The right not to be present. The right not to be funny. The right to be cynical. The right to have bad days. The right to wake up late. The right to be late picking Melvil up from the nursery. The right to mess up the 'home-made' meals I try to make. The right not to be in a good mood. The right not to reveal everything. The right not to talk about it any more. The right to be ordinary. The right to be afraid. The right not to know. The right not to want. The right not to be capable.

TIDYING UP
HER THINGS

22 November
11 p.m.

Everything is in its right place. From the laundry basket, I take the last things of hers that still bear her scent. I press them against my face every night, so that I can fall asleep with that smell of eternity. But nothing else has moved. I can't. And yet the funeral is in two days and I must choose the clothes she will wear. I wish she could stay naked. I wish I could slip into the coffin with her, both of us naked. And let them close the lid so we can finally warm each other up.

My hand touches the fabrics hanging in the wardrobe. Each material is a memory. The wool of her long coat is a walk through the forest one winter morning. Her nose is red, her eyes peer over her glasses. She has one hand in her pocket, the other in my hand. Hélène lived in the present. She gave herself entirely to the moments that she lived. We had a bench that was ours in those woods. That was where I asked her to marry me. She pretended to be surprised.

Under a plastic cover, a light tulle skirt, slightly off-white. Time has darkened it. It was the skirt she wore the first time we kissed. The veils danced around her. Like butterflies caught in a net. She was a dancer in a music box. This will be the one. Soon, under the gravestone, surrounded by envious corpses, a little dancer will wait for her box to be opened. From above, Melvil and I will hear the music play.

On a shelf, the cotton of her T-shirts. Relics of youthful freedom, lived for music. Led Zeppelin, the Misfits, Sleater-Kinney, the Cramps, the Ramones . . . she wore rock 'n' roll like a badge of honour. Transcended by the riffs and the rhythms that beat inside her head. No posturing. No pretending. When Hélène let you into her bubble, you felt privileged. Chosen by a soul who gave herself without restraint. I was the one to whom she gave everything. The king of her world.

Higher up, I grab a brightly coloured shirt: happy orange, with little white checks. She would tie the hem around her hips, exposing the lower part of her belly that I kissed so many times.

She was summer. Warm, alive, sometimes crushed by an oppressive heatwave. Sometimes threatened by an evening storm. But a season of freedom. In summer, the nights are short. We feel like loving.

Right at the top, boxes belonging to a collection that was just getting started: her formal shoes, her stilettos. Heels so high they seemed to go on for ever. Leather laces up to her ankle, boots that were not made for walking. Hélène was a bird-woman, slender and light, and her shoes slept in their boxes most of the time. And yet I can still hear them echoing on the floorboards. One love-filled morning, half naked, when she put them on just for the pleasure of wearing them. It didn't matter that no

one saw them except me. She didn't care about the
rest of the world. She was the fulcrum of ours.
Everything revolved around her. The moon was our
planet. We were its only two inhabitants.

On her dressing table, the lid is still missing from
the tube of mascara, her glasses left casually aside,
awaiting her return. She thought she was plain. So
she wore make-up.

She would spend hours in front of that mirror,
getting ready to go out. The ritual was skilfully organised. Preparing her skin, then the foundation,
eyes, mouth, and finally the blush on her cheeks. It
was a spectacle. And, like an actor putting on her
costume, she became someone else with the mask of
light in place. The gentle, reserved young woman
became a majestic lady.

I loved them both equally. One lived in the other.
She was the two of them, together.

In the bathroom, perfectly aligned in rows, her
bottles of perfume. They bear the names of sensual-
ity: Louve, Bas de Soie, Datura Noir. I can still taste

it in my mouth, when I kissed her stretched-out body. Her mouth was cool, her breasts were soft, her back slightly arched, her hips accentuated. Together, we learned to love.

Louve was her favourite.

On the bed, her clothes are placed as they will be when she is buried. As I spray them with perfume, I seem to see them rise up. On the lifeless fabric, little by little, her body appears. Her fragile shoulders, her legs, her hands, her buttocks, her breasts. She is there, all mine.

I lie next to that invisible body. Her breath caresses my neck. She embraces me. Puts her hand on my face. Tells me that everything will be all right. This is the last time we will be able to love each other.

LETTER FROM

MELVIL

24 November
4 p.m.

The day of the funeral. Melvil is too young to come with me. I am alone before a swarm of sadness. I don't want to talk, I have already said too much. So I lend my words to he who does not yet have any, my voice to he whose voice cannot be heard. I no longer am. I am him.

> *Mama,*
> *I am writing you this note to tell you that I love you. I miss you. Papa is helping me because I'm still very young. Don't worry about him —*
> *I'll look after him. I take him for walks, we play*

with my little cars, we read stories, we take baths together and we have lots of hugs. It's not the same as it was when you were there, but it's okay. He tells me everything will be all right, but I can tell he's sad. I am sad too.

The other night, we looked at photos of you on the phone. We listened to your song too. We cried a lot. Papa told me you won't be able to come and see me any more. He also told me that we were a team now, the two of us. A team of adventurers. I liked that idea because Papa was really smiling when he said it. Because recently when he's smiled at me, it's as if he were crying.

Papa told me that we'll get by, and that when things aren't going well, we will think about you because you'll be there, with us. He asked all your friends to write me a letter that I'll be able to read when I'm older. He told me we weren't the only ones who loved you, but that no one else loved you as much as we did. He also told me that children do not have memories before they are three, but that the seventeen months I spent with you will make me the man I will become.

There have been lots of things happening around us recently. I think it's partly because of Papa, but he didn't do it on purpose. There are ladies who stop us in the street to say hello, the telephone never stops ringing, and I get presents from people I don't even know. I tell him it doesn't matter, that you always loved us as we were and that you would have forgiven him for all of that.

You have to forgive me too because I couldn't be here today. You know me — I don't like it when there are too many grown-ups. And Papa told me it took a long time and it was cold. But Papa also promised me that we would come to see you tomorrow, the two of us.

Okay, well, I can't wait to see you tomorrow, and the day after tomorrow, and all the days after that. I miss you, Mama. I love you.

Melvil

THE END OF
THE STORY

24 November
10 p.m.

I started writing this book the day after I posted the letter on Facebook, maybe even that same evening. Whenever Melvil is in nursery, I sit at my computer to disgorge all these words that live inside my head. Like the neighbours upstairs who listen to music too loud. I type them on my keyboard to quieten them, so they will stop fighting and let me sleep.

As soon as they appear on the screen, I look at them like foreign bodies, I read them to understand them, I reread them to understand myself, and end up loving them. I watch them from afar, holding hands. Sometimes I try to call out to them, but my voice doesn't reach them. The words don't belong to me any more.

I had to write quickly. I am the one who loves Hélène, not the one who loved her. Before death drops the curtain down on the person I was, without a final encore, I am still this naive fool prevented from falling by hope. Who knows what I'll become tomorrow, when my grief has let me fall?

Like a brief, fleeting love, an all-consuming passion, it is just passing by. A vivid reflection of the love that shone so brightly. It is beautiful, intense, I hold it tight against me. But I know that it has almost left me already.

In search of another lover to torment, it goes on its way, abandoning me to its sad travelling companion. Mourning.

I spot its mark, a grey stain that appears on my side. I have already seen it grow, in the same place, a few years ago, when I lost my mother. This one is darker. It spreads faster too. It is only a question of days, weeks now; I am besieged. It covers almost the whole of my stomach. I no longer feel like doing anything. Eating is torture.

Soon it will insinuate itself into my chest, press against my thorax to prevent me from breathing. Penetrating what remains of my heart, it will discharge its death-coloured venom through all of my veins and arteries. My legs will no longer be able to hold me up, my knees will lock in place and my feet will turn to clay. It will drag down on my shoulders to make them slump, and I won't be able to lift my arms. My body will abandon me, but there will still be my mind. Given a suspended sentence, so I can watch myself sink.

But I am not afraid. I am waiting for it, I know it. Sometimes I try to convince myself to be patient, but the grey stain is remorseless, meticulous. From the base of my neck, it will rise at last up my throat, its grip growing tighter and tighter. My nose will no longer be able to recognise the smell of a memory. My eyes will see only what is in front of them.

I would have liked my first book to be a story, not mine. I would have liked to love the words without fearing them.

There have been times when, as someone else whose opinion I have sought has read out loud the words I typed on my computer, it seemed to me as if I were discovering those words, hearing them for the first time. I was almost surprised to find out how difficult life was going to be for those two little guys. I wanted to help them. I loved them too, the pair of them. With their ladybirds and their supermarket meals and the nursery ladies who will never replace Mama.

I couldn't tell a story. That was not how things appeared to me. I have no beginning, no end, and every hour overwhelms my entire being. My present must become past, and I drift through this everyday life without time, through these days without hours.

Since Hélène's death, there is no tale to tell. It's the end of the story. There are only these instants that rise up, taking me by surprise. It was these moments I had to write about, Polaroids of a life that has not yet got its breath back.

I await that evening when, my face already darkened, I press my still-pink lips to my son's forehead as he lies in bed. One last kiss from the man I was, the one who loved his mother like no other, the one who saw him born, eyes open to the world, the one who dreamed of a life where they would take the time to love each other. The last moment of our life before.

When he falls asleep that night, I will abandon myself completely to darkness.

Tomorrow, we will go to see his mother. This book is almost finished.

It will not heal me. No one can be healed of death. All they can do is tame it. Death is a wild animal, sharp-fanged. I am just trying to build a cage to keep it locked in. It is there, beside me, drooling as it waits to devour me. The bars of the cage that protect me are made of paper. When I turn off the computer, the beast is released.

MAMA IS THERE

25 November
7.45 a.m.

Melvil has just guzzled down the contents of his bottle. He hasn't lost his appetite. He sits between my legs and we savour the early-morning calm in the still-warm bed. We both try to prolong the pleasure. I softly hum songs to him. He lists all the elements of my face: 'Papa's nose', 'Papa's mouth', 'Where are Papa's ears?' Neither of us wants to leave the comfort of that morning.

We have to get ready, get washed. Before, a shower was just a shower: hot water, soap, shampoo. This morning, it is an adventure, and Melvil is the hero. And the villain of the story is the showerhead, a strange metal face that spits hot, smoking liquid from its many mouths, making Papa its prisoner. Melvil must do everything he can to liberate me from this curse. He paces around outside the bathroom, coming up with a plan of attack.

Leaving the door open enables him to combat the smoke, which flees instantly.

'Melvil, close the door, I'm cold!'

First victory.

Putting his hands, his arms, his hair, anything he can, under the water seems to accelerate Papa's liberation.

'You're going to get all wet . . . Get out of the bathroom!'

Second victory.

Going away and being silent is the only way to be called back into battle.

'Melvil, where are you, sweetie? Come here!'

Third victory.

But his secret weapon is the picture book. The metal snake stops spitting as soon as it goes in the bath.

'No, don't put the book in the water!'

The fatal blow is delivered. The battle is over.

I break down. I lose it. Tears flood my face. Today, we are going to his mother's grave.

———

Yesterday, Melvil did not go to the funeral. Too cold, too long, too tough for a little boy. Anyway, this is a moment that we must go through alone. Before going to the funeral, I told him everything. That his mama was going to be buried, that our memories would live with us but that her body would remain down there. I also promised him that we would go to see her the next day.

And yet, today, the closer the moment draws, the more afraid I am. Afraid that he won't understand. Afraid that he'll understand everything. Afraid that I haven't prepared him properly. Afraid that I've told him too much. But we have to go.

His eyes like two marbles, he looks at me forgivingly. He knows it is not the wet book that is making me cry. He tries to take the burden of all I can no longer carry. 'But you're too little for that, my love.' A wet hug is enough to reassure him, to reassure me.

We have to get ready. In an intimate silence, we go through the stages of our morning routine, one by one. Nappy, clothes, shoes, jacket, hug. He knows this is not just an ordinary day.

I bring the photo of her and him. I will place it on the headstone so he understands that Mama is there. They are beautiful. Even though there is a drawing of a rocket on it, the dummy does not leave Melvil's mouth. His head leans gently towards her so his cheek touches hers. Just the faintest touch, enough to feel her presence. She looks serene, smiling inwardly, eyes trusting. The time is ours. We are on holiday.

Closing the door of the flat that day is like leaving a life behind us. From now on, it will be strange to us. A place where we no longer live. A place where it feels as if we never lived. Like a little house inside us, full of familiar smells, rituals and habits, a place we love, a place we feel at ease, but we can never go in there again.

We knocked, scratched at the door, tried to smash it down, but Hélène is locked in, alone in our empty house. The key is with her, buried in Division X of Montmartre Cemetery.

The weather is mild today. A cloud scatters and sunlight pours down on the cemetery like honey flowing from the sky. Only yesterday, it was blood that fell from the clouds. An icy blood that pounded in time with our footsteps against the crowd of um-brellas that filled the wide path. Today, the funeral procession is over. It is towards our new life that we walk.

Melvil holds my hand. His head barely reaches the middle of my thigh, but he looks so big. He has fun jumping in a puddle left by the rain. Little by little, my fear is diluted in the water that noisily splashes as he stamps his feet in it. The game is his weapon, the next bout of silliness his horizon. A child is not weighed down by grown-up things. His innocence is our reprieve.

Left after the central square, that's where her tomb is. We approach it. We are there. My whole life lies below my feet. Held in a few square metres of stone, cold and mud. It's a small thing, a life. I put the photograph in the middle of the white flowers that spangle the gravestone. Like a swarm of stars hung in the night sky. A moonless night. Locked in her vault, she will never reappear.

'Mama is there.'

Suddenly Melvil lets go of my hand. He climbs on the gravestone, crushing the roses and the lilies that are no match for his determination. I am afraid he is looking for her. He keeps going through the jungle of regrets. Grabs the photo. Takes it with him. Then comes back to me, and holds my hand. I know he has found her.

He wants to leave. Right away. No hanging around. He wants to take Mama back home with us. I don't resist. He wants arms around him. I hold him tight against me. She is with us. There are three of us. There will always be three of us.

On our way out, I see the puddle. I hop into it. He laughs.

penguin.co.uk/vintage